HOW TO AVOID THE PITFALLS OF NONPROFIT

HELL

Doña Keating

∞ Dedication ∞

To my mum, dad, sisters, husband, and daughter: the only people in the multiverse who can infuriate me beyond human comprehension and still command my genuine, deep, and eternal love.

Do try this one at home...

Acknowledgments

There are so many who've assisted me in this undertaking without knowing it, whether through their actions, or lack thereof. I thank you.

I'd especially thank my husband Charles for the extra pair of brilliant eyes which pored over my thoughts and correctly presumed my intentions when offering input. Also, Ted Farmer and Charles Huff, dear and insightful friends who provided suggestions based on their numerous professional successes. And to my friend Dr. Nancy Harkrider, an internationally renowned and respected author, speaker, consultant, and fellow world traveler.

Thank you all for being there for me

when it mattered.

Disclaimer

This book is presented for educational and informational purposes. The author and publisher are not offering it as legal, accounting, or other professional services advice outside of its purview; no representations or warranties of any kind are made; author and publisher assume no liabilities of any kind with respect to the accuracy or completeness of the contents; and neither shall be held liable or responsible to any person or entity with respect to any loss or incidental or consequential damages caused, or alleged to have been caused, directly or indirectly, by the information or programs contained herein. Every company is different and the advice and strategies contained herein may not be suitable for your situation. You should seek the services of a competent professional before beginning any improvement programme.

Facebook.com/ProfessionalOptions
Twitter.com/profoptions
DonaKeating.com
ISBN:978-1478171041
ISBN:1478171049

Foreword

This will not be your typical "how to" book. Then again, perhaps it is when one considers how social media has catapulted interactions into hyper-informal frontiers where direct and bolshie commentary is de rigueur.

The goal is to offer valuable observations and solutions borne of decades of service on non-profit boards and committees, advising them, or facilitating executive retreats. You'll pardon the occasionally pithy tone, though I suspect you're here because you've walked this path and appreciate how fire can burn off layers of dead skin to reveal new and improved determination and focus. In which case, the invitation to share a collective scream into a pillow will give rise to the real focus: getting past the drama into effective board leadership and participation.

As with anything, take what works and leave the rest behind. At the very least, this missive might provide validation, food for thought, or kick start meaningful conversations towards fruitful and effective results. If you see yourself in any of this, perhaps the reality check will inspire you to reconsider your approach - thus adding years to the collective lives of your fellow directors.

-----Table of Contents-----

I.   The Basics

I choose not to belabour the following subject. Not because it isn't important - it is indeed critical - but there are thousands of resources which serve this topic in depth. Just not where I choose to go today, though that could change. Tag along and see where it all leads.

Taking the necessary steps to build organisational infrastructure and memory is both prudent and life-preserving. Not only will it reduce frustration and directionless policy, but this process leads to greater clarity when conducting business and expressing your value proposition to stakeholders, members, and the community being served.

Speaking of clarity, what we're referring to are things like bylaws, charters, and standard operating guidelines, so virtually anyone can step in and run the nonprofit if everyone perishes in a nuclear blast. Communications/social media, how to set up and run meetings, membership, programme and events, committees (or what we call working groups so as not to frighten phobes or attract process drones), special interest groups, volunteer management, fundraising, board or sponsor/member recruitment,

board orientation....if it's an

intrinsic or core aspect of governing,

managing, or executing on your mission,

create and refine these as appropriate.

I'll revisit some mechanics and other

thoughts around this later.

II.   Who

This is a question too many boards don't bother to answer or understand. And if they do, it's conveniently disregarded. Volunteer leadership on nonprofit boards is hard work and sometimes thankless. And yet, it is a resume builder which attracts both the well-meaning and egotistical.

Nevertheless, decide who you want to be. Are you an executive or governing board which wants to focus on policy and setting the direction of the organization? Or, are you a working board which will attend to administration and even hands on duties? This decision will, of course,

be impacted by the nature and size of

your entity. However, there is a school

of thought that all nonprofit boards

are ultimately working boards because

both versions involve, well -- work. I

grok[1] that semantic, but the reality is

----

[1] To grok (play /ˈgrɒk/) is to intimately and completely share the same reality or line of thinking with another physical or conceptual entity. Author Robert A. Heinlein coined the term in his best-selling 1961 book Stranger in a Strange Land. In Heinlein's view, grokking is the intermingling of intelligence that necessarily affects both the observer and the observed. From the novel:

Grok means to understand so thoroughly that the observer becomes a part of the observed—to merge, blend, intermarry, lose identity in group experience. It means almost everything that we mean by religion, philosophy, and science—and it means as little to us (because of our Earthling assumptions) as color means to a blind man.

The Oxford English Dictionary defines grok as "to understand intuitively or by empathy; to establish rapport with" and "to empathise or communicate sympathetically (with); also, to experience enjoyment". Other forms of the word include groks (present third person singular), grokked (past participle) and grokking (present participle).

In an ideological context, a grokked concept becomes part of the person who contributes to its evolution by improving the doctrine, perpetuating the myth, espousing the belief, adding detail to the

too many boards become ineffective or
frustrated when directors micromanage,
or get lost (perhaps even hide) in
process to the degree where achieving
measurable results is compromised.

If you've chosen the
governing/executive route, build the
necessary volunteer or paid team to
carry out the vision. Absent human or
financial capital, craft a commitment
statement which realistically describes
needs, expectations, and
responsibilities. Should your
logistical makeup call for a hands-on
board, use retreats to self-review and

social plan, refining the idea or proving the theory.
http://en.wikipedia.org/wiki/Grok

calibrate at the 30,000 foot level, and encourage input from advisors and other community stakeholders who can provide needed perspective.

III. Why

Know your mission and target audience. Conduct honest and solutions-oriented discussions towards a better understanding of how to get there.

More importantly, the why here is about your decision to join the board. Building your curriculum vitae is a reasonable endeavour. Joining a board for primarily this purpose, then abandoning your responsibilities and forcing officers or the board chairperson to chase you down to do what you've promised to do, is not.

You know they need you because it's a volunteer undertaking. Thus, you place these individuals in the position of imploring, persuading, groveling, begging...and all sorts of organisational management tricks and tools they've learned over the years. Meanwhile, they're seething underneath because your unspoken message of presumed superiority has chipped away at group morale and consumed time no one can afford to waste. Now the task of entreating your cooperation has leeched into keeping those engaged who resent investing their time when you can get away with neglecting your valued role.

We all get busy and the unexpected
occurs, but please do yourself and
everyone a favour and give your tenure
on the board the serious consideration
it deserves. If you can't do what you
initially thought you could, work with
the group to identify pieces you can
realistically handle. In the event you
must part ways, try not to justify it
in a fit of self-righteous pique after
passive-aggressively creating the need
for one too many emphatic reminders.

I'm not splitting the atom here: much
of what we're addressing is
straightforward, and understood on some
level by the majority of board members
I've encountered. Keep the benefit of

service and the end product in the
forefront of your psyche, particularly
when you feel the least like doing so.
Stay clear on why you chose to serve
and bring your skills and gifts to the
bountiful table. Don't hesitate to ask
for help when you need it.

IV.   Typical Hell-Inducing Scenarios

Be it your time, money, or
ambassadorship, commitment as a board
member is vitally important to the
heartbeat of a nonprofit organisation.
Unfortunately, there are instances
where boards and its members fall
short. I've listed a few of the most
common below, but have also offered
suggestions which can put the wheels
back on the track.

Founder's Syndrome

This will typically apply to newer
organisations, although there are

instances of this with entities which have been around for many years.

We've all seen it: an influential, visionary, and bright leader who helped found the nonprofit. Either s/he won't go away or relinquish the reigns when it's clearly time to do so, or they have moved on but reach back in to ensure 'their baby' is being cared for in a manner they deem warranted. Of course, a delicate line must be walked between telling him or her to hoof it and diplomatically indulging their input…particularly if they wield significant influence.

Ironically, I've seen very few cases of this in my career. When I did, it was always an ugly affair with founders threatening to persuade friends to cease financial support of the nonprofit in question. A rather foolish move when one considers how this would impact the ability to continue providing needed or valued services to the intended community.

If you find yourself in the position of witnessing the decline of an organisation you started - this is not to be confused with ire that your fiefdom has ended - sit down in a sincere discussion with the board chair. Should you be in the position to help by recruiting additional staff, directors, or donating money, commit to at least one of these steps before offering to micromanage from the omniscient perch of an advisory council position.

There is a flip side to Founder's Syndrome, and I know it well from both personal experience and observation. This is a situation where the founder(s) are almost desperate for intelligent, visionary, and accountable leadership to take the reins so s/he may move on. Instead, there is a revolving door of directors who begin as quite well-intentioned and revved up individuals, rife with promises about what they'll bring to the table. Over time, it becomes apparent neither talent nor will is present, much less resilience. This is also where one learns of those who joined to polish up the CV.

When the realisation hits, a founder who actually cares about meeting mission objectives will spend time coaxing follow-through from those who've repeatedly dropped the ball, or adopted criticism or process in lieu of execution. Under these circumstances, it isn't unusual for founders to take on more tasks or curtail time-wasting actions in favour of 'executive decisions', thereby earning a Founder's Syndrome charge. In actuality, that founder has accepted s/he will be left holding the bag and opted for two weeks' notice versus two days.

If you're truly guilty of this syndrome
and know it, pivot that energy into a
more helpful role so the current leader
and board can succeed with mission-
critical efforts. Should you be the
rare person who is oblivious to your
status as an interloper, ask a
straightforward friend or colleague and
suck in your breath to prepare for the
blow. For those who unfairly tag
leaders with this label to escape the
truth of their less than present or
effective leadership, try some deep
introspection and ownership.
Organisations are sustainable when they
have the resources to continue
meaningful work. If you're not part of

moving the momentum forward, you're a
hindrance and part of the problem.
Shape up or ship out.

No Shows

Few things are more debilitating to an
entity than directors who disengage.
Failing to show up for meetings,
events, calls, or follow through on
commitments is the single most
frustrating complaint I've heard from
nonprofit leadership.

You might not be paid for your nonprofit service, but there is a team
relying on your presence and input to

sustain operations. No shows, especially without notice, are rude and show a lack of respect for other members and their time. You are no more important than they are, and it is challenging for a board chair or president to congeal the rest of the team when other members are seemingly given a pass.

Life can be unpredictable – with events, meetings, and family emergencies which call us away without notice. Nonetheless, a text, call, or quick email to inform your fellow members is a basic common courtesy...particularly for those only too eager to announce on Facebook what their dog had for dinner.

Process Over Action

Ego is prevalent in leadership, and nonprofit boards are no exception. While some directors are more than ready to jump in and execute on historically documented vision, others believe it imperative to 'improve' or 'change' the status quo – even if it's working – so they can go away with an imagined feather in their cap. As a result, board members are subjected to an endless stream of document review, planning sessions, and discussion surrounding the nonprofit's infrastructure, vision, or mission –

with little actually getting done. This is also a tactic used by board members who knew they signed up for a working board environment, but have decided along the way they don't want to roll up their sleeves. Directors exhausted by this time-consuming exercise no longer have the desire to participate, and forward movement is stunted.

The next time you decide to dazzle the board by taking a page from the Arthur Anderson playbook[2], think again. Does

---

[2] **Arthur Andersen LLP,** based in Chicago, was once one of the "Big Five" accounting firms among PricewaterhouseCoopers, Deloitte Touche Tohmatsu, Ernst & Young and KPMG, providing auditing, tax, and consulting services to large corporations. In 2002, the firm voluntarily surrendered its licenses to practice as Certified Public Accountants in the United States after being found guilty of criminal charges relating to the firm's handling of the auditing of Enron, an energy corporation based in Texas, which had filed for bankruptcy in 2001 and later failed. The other national accounting and consulting

your information *really* deliver the substance of the lofty subject matter it portends to explore? Or, does it instead represent a comparatively minor dent in the organisation's oeuvre?

There is no doubt new board members can be a great asset by introducing new ideas and tweaking old assumptions. However, a constantly changing landscape can be as destructive as arteriosclerotic bureaucracy, and ultimately, too much navel-gazing can

---

firms bought most of the practices of Arthur Andersen. The verdict was subsequently overturned by the Supreme Court of the United States. However, the damage to its reputation has prevented it from returning as a viable business, though it still nominally exists. (http://en.wikipedia.org/wiki/Arthur_Andersen)

A common description of its work was unnecessary wordiness, as best exemplified in an internet joke entitled "Why Did the Chicken Cross the Road?" (see http://askville.amazon.com/chicken-cross-road/AnswerViewer.do?requestId=807569)

lead to running in place. Balance must be struck between meaningful input and analysis paralysis, or nitpicking which merely rearranges the deck chairs without providing much that is comparatively new, inspiring, or relevant to the entity's bottom line.

Swiss Cheese Orientation

In an increasingly technological world, it's tempting to zip or email documents to board members about your entity when they initially join. Unfortunately, only the really attentive directors will review them; much less place them in an accessible folder structure for ongoing reference. The other

alternative is the ever-growing binders
and folders kept by the corporate
secretary, who is less likely to know
where relevant documents are unless
they, too, are well-organised and
attentive.

The net effect is a poorly informed
board which regularly asks questions
about documented policies, procedures
and guidelines it should already know.
Or, an aggravating cycle of assuming,
by default, that what they're unaware
of must not exist as an aspect of the
organisation's infrastructure. This can
also lead to process over action,
wherein existing documents are pored
over with a fine tooth comb and

rewritten while other significant deadlines and tasks are neglected.

There are many tools which provide a space in the cloud for uploading and sharing large documents. Notwithstanding its use, board chairs should make every effort to create a binder of relevant documents and templates, which should be given to new board members upon joining. Set aside an hour or so to meet and discuss the contents, or answer any questions which may arise. If several new members have been elected or appointed, schedule a retreat to strategise and reaffirm important information about the organisation.

Speaking of retreats, I could write an entire section about this alone: dos and don'ts, scheduling the agenda, ensuring there is a third party facilitator, and powering through ad nauseum brainstorming sessions into action items with measurable goals.

Rambling Meetings

This is a rather straightforward proposition. All meetings should be framed by an agenda. Wherever possible, status or committee reports can be forwarded prior to convening so discussions aren't in the weeds. More importantly, ensure your meeting has a defined purpose, or clarity regarding the goals you'd like to sketch out and achieve. If there are minutes or notes, provide them ahead of time so board members have an opportunity to review and come prepared with input or questions. Allot specific timeframes for each item so tangential straying doesn't compromise what should be a strategic session. Don't be afraid to firmly but gently redirect discussion back on course. Last but certainly not least, start and end on time – and prepare a parking lot list for matters which can be tabled for another time.

Now that we're all nodding in agreement
about these tenets, why are we
simultaneously recalling occurrences
where members arrived late or not at
all; came unprepared; commandeered
meetings; allowed them to devolve into
gelatinous blobs of pseudo-purpose; or
simply had no bloody idea why we were
even meeting?

If you're a board chair who has allowed
this to occur, tighten your belt and
exhibit some leadership by bringing
these basics back into the fold.
Failure to do so indicates a lack of
respect for the time and commitment of
your board members, and can lead to
decisions on their part to avoid or

minimise future attendance. And of course, if you're that ill-prepared, domineering, pontificating, or late/no-show member, the message you send is you're more important than other directors. Further, your blasé attitude can become infectious, thereby jeopardising overall board and mission effectiveness.

In all cases, airing out underlying grievances or issues can pave the way for productive, inclusive, and engaged meetings.

The Critic

Construction criticism is healthy and a tool for ongoing improvement. Though

it can be difficult to take, it's
important to actively listen to what is
being said so a helpful dialogue can
then ensue. What usually happens is the
subject becomes offended, and the
exchange becomes confrontational.

However, more important is the
deleterious impact of The Critic in
this setting. Why? Because more often
than not, the individual in question
has chosen this path over that of
active doer. When work is required,
they are too busy or conveniently
unreachable. Once it's completed, they
are front and centre - full blown *deus
ex machina* syndrome intact - swooping
down to save the board from itself with

a slew of ultimately inconsequential post-project corrections or complaints. An already overburdened board or leader will obviously resent this approach, particularly if you were the board member charged with the responsibility.

Again, there is legitimate benefit in value judgments and an honest critique towards polished results, but it is disingenuous at best to adopt this modus operandi without timely contributions *before* the work is completed. I've seen fist fights and shoving matches in board rooms because of it, and it can breed resentment or a demoralised environment.

There is a poignant saying: "Those who say it cannot be done should not interrupt those who are doing it." Enough said.

Obstructionism

The saying in the preceding scenario was a spot on softball and lead-in for this one.

How many of us have witnessed boards in the midst of endlessly fractious relations, complete with waste deep (deliberate spelling) - rogue on a mission to delay or obstruct a decision with which they disagree? We could also tag this one 'sore loser'.

Another variation on the theme is when an ego-driven director self-appoints him or herself an expert on a topic, then holds the rest of the board hostage by attempting to change or 'update' everything previously reviewed and decided. This is less about delivering a viable end product, and more about the ability to (falsely) represent oneself as the saviour who got the nonprofit back on track. Not only is it rubbish, but this consumes time which could be better spent on mission-critical strategies and deadlines.

The bottom line here: unless a fiduciary body is involved in illegal activity – or that which violates policy or the public good, a majority or quorum resolution should proceed with a single body voice. An ossified mindset impedes deliberations, and while it is reasonable to state objections, don't sabotage to the detriment of the board and organisation's accomplishments once the board has approved an action, policy, or decision.

If obstructionists cannot reform or consider the benefits to the larger body, they undermine the mission of the organisation and must go.

Overpromise, Under-deliver

The majority of those who make the decision to serve on nonprofit boards will have the best interests of the organisation at heart. Excitement about joining is at its highest peak, and the mind races with the possibilities of what can be achieved with the team. What usually works best is to under promise and over deliver so results are magnified and expectations, managed.

Unfortunately, too many board members sign up for a list of initiatives and actions, then fizzle out and deliver a marginal work product – or nothing at all. Not only does this frustrate board chairs and other active members, but it can set operations back weeks or months, sometimes more.

The saying 'If you want something done, ask a busy person to do it' is one of those truths which initially seems counterintuitive. 'Wouldn't you want to instead give it to the person with more time on their hands?' you might ask. Until one realises there's a good reason busy people are in high demand. It's not because they're circus freaks who enjoy performing the octopus juggle; they're the sort willing to make sacrifices, go the extra mile, and ensure the vision is executed. Failure, for them, is simply not an option - and because they are busy, it's likely they'll appreciate the value of time, theirs and others, and not want to waste it.

While tempting to stack the board with those who claim they can devote time because they're not busy, consider that once they find a new job or the going gets tough, there will suddenly be more reasons for their unavailability or failure to produce. That isn't to say, however, many retirees or otherwise more available candidates can't bring excellence and quality input to the board, because many do.

There is, of course, a caveat. Too much dumping on high performers becomes an ultimately destructive habit. They'll burn out, become resentful, or the occasional thing might slip through the cracks. If this member is the organisation's leader, this can lead to self-protective actions which result in unfair charges of Founders Syndrome, and incites a cycle of criticism from directors trying to deflect or hide their own lackluster contributions.

Delegating and involving other team members is a well-rounded approach which strengthens and empowers the board to successfully represent the entity and its community base. It also

pays to calibrate or reframe so members
are recruited who can successfully
gauge their contributions, and use
well-developed time management skills
to ensure commitments translate into
real and meaningful work.

Silos

In today's economy, businesses are
tightening their belts due to declining
revenues. For non-profits, many grant
funding sources have begun to dry up.
This state of affairs intensifies the
need to establish and sustain value
proposition. It is also a prime
opportunity to revisit efficiencies of

scale and streamline operations while returning to core mission.

Other mechanisms for remaining viable include partnerships or collaboration with similar or complementary organisations. For some non-profit board members, this is the first step towards walking the plank to irrelevancy or extinction, and all weapons are amassed for a full on assault against those who recommend this option.

In a Web 2.0 world, silo cultures and turf wars are walls which stymie internal and external communication.

Opportunities to present a stronger local, regional, or statewide front are increased when entities can pool or share resources.

From an internal perspective, forcing community clients to drudge through the centralised model of 'departments' or rigid protocols constrains the ability to share knowledge or incorporate mobile and adaptive expertise. As a general principle, a more transparent and cooperative ethos will improve an entity's effectiveness and long-term sustainability.

Remember: if you insist on swimming
alone, there's no one nearby to save
you if you begin to drown.

Taking Toys and Going Home

This could be an offshoot of any one of
the hell-inducing scenarios discussed
above. Or, a member wielding
significant power, influence, or money.
It can be a single director or a subset
of the board.

The wound is created during a specific
meeting or series thereof, where a
slight is perceived. It is further
picked and festers in sidebar meetings

where sub-teams grouse about their projected dissatisfaction. Whether the grievance is real or imagined, the board is subjected to passive-aggressive or coliseum like jousts between those angling for power.

Blood, blood everywhere, and not a mop in sight. Before anyone can inject sanity, the disgruntled members take their toys and go home. No more money or advocacy on the nonprofit's behalf. Corporate records are returned months later out of spite. Letters to the Editor crop up to criticise or undermine the organisation or its leaders, and gossip is spread throughout the community to ensure the sandbox is no longer usable by anyone other than Baby Huey[3]. Those who know better will choose to make informed opinions, but others will jump on the bandwagon and fan the flames of toxified public opinion.

If you're storming off in a tantrum from the board, ask yourself if you truly want to do damage to an organisation with a worthy cause

---

[3] Baby Huey is a gigantic and naïve duckling cartoon character. He was created by Martin Taras for Paramount Pictures' Famous Studios, and became a Paramount cartoon star during the 1950s. Although created by Famous for its animated cartoons, Huey first appeared in comic-book form in an original story in *Casper the Friendly Ghost* #1 September 1949, as published by St. John Publications. Many animated shorts featuring Huey had recurring themes. Most common among them was him trying to be just like any other kid his age. He would see his peers playing, and would immediately get excited. Whenever he tried to involve himself in the activities of his peers (also anthropomorphic ducklings) he would often inadvertently cause more problems, and as a result they would drive him away through trickery (and into tears). (see http://en.wikipedia.org/wiki/Baby_Huey)

because your opinions weren't the final decision or not enough people kissed your ring. Does disrupting business continuity benefit the community being served?

Time to take some deep breaths, look squarely in the mirror, and be a professional who provides sufficient notice along with transitional assistance to your successor.

What Have You Done For Me Lately?

No matter how much you bring to the table, fellow directors or board chairs insist upon explaining every aspect of nonprofit leadership or organisational dynamics. Previous successes don't matter, and board members are placed in the position of having to prove themselves anew or repeatedly describe their knowledge and experience. This unfortunate scenario can be due to ego or a tendency to micromanage.

Some level of orientation for board members is both necessary and important, but so is knowing your audience. Getting clear on the capabilities of your team and team members will save time and reduce dissatisfaction. Thoroughly review board member applications and resumes when undergoing the recruitment

process, and allow sufficient time for
an exchange of ideas during board
meetings and retreats. Directors are
there to help, not be treated like
brain dead zombies.

Resume Dropper

This is the flip side of the previous
scenario, wherein directors believe
their prior experience renders them
omniscient. Other director's ideas are
either stupid or subordinate, and more
time is spent on what they achieved at
nonprofit XYZ, how many awards,
certificates or degrees were acquired,
and the grateful minions who
genuflected.

Accolades matter, but form without function doesn't get the job done. There is no room on a nonprofit board for a prima donna, particularly if they aren't prolific. Respect what each member brings to the organisation, and capitalise on strengths to create a well-oiled machine.

Stacking the Deck

Similar to Founder's Syndrome, a powerful Executive Director with extensive history not only believes they *are* the organisation, but loads the board with their directors without checks and balances from existing directors or stakeholder members.

Bowing to legacy might seem like a safe route, but it compromises operational integrity, and creates lockstep leadership which can become sluggish.

The election or appointment process for board members should be articulated in the bylaws and carried out objectively. Form a committee to recruit and vet candidates, review applications, and submit finalists for further action.

All Hammers and No Saws

Usually, when diversity is introduced as a necessary component of well-functioning boards, the reference is to token racial placements or public appeals to selected demographics the organisation serves. The value of reaching a significant or relevant contingent shouldn't be ignored, but presuming such a candidate will automatically address this need based on surface appearances or presumed similarities can backfire.

More important are board members who bring a wide range of valuable expertise to the board. Law, finance/accounting, business, entrepreneurial, process or organisational management, communications, fundraising, and compliance are just some examples of the critical skillsets which bring effective representation to nonprofit boards.

It is an unfortunate circumstance that we don't always get to be choosy regarding who shows up for board service, especially in smaller organisations. Here it is best to extract the cream from the crop of applicants.

The Relentless Face

Whether a founder, executive director, president or CEO of a nonprofit, this is the self-appointed individual who has decided they are the face and sole spokesperson for the nonprofit.

Collateral is saturated with their visage and thoughts, and power struggles with the board or board chair typically occur regarding who should be the official envoy.

While it is true the general public or constituent base prefers the personal or human touch of an individual versus an entity, running a successful nonprofit is a team effort. Communities thrive when both board members and executive directors are engaged and visible. Identify opportunities where everyone can step up and play a valued role.

All Chiefs, No Indians

I'm not a fan of this politically incorrect title, though it is illustrative of the need to create a well-balanced board with not only leadership but understanding. As we've acknowledged, nonprofits attract board members who want to make a difference. It's a good thing to have members with passion for your mission, but a side effect of highly motivated leaders is strong ideas with egos to match. Not necessarily bad, but if a member disregards board orientation efforts and materials and declares they have the solution, the challenge is in keeping everyone on task instead of retreading. The prudent leader will

63

take the time to understand the entity's history, why something was done or tabled, and other information or data which can illuminate next steps. It is also tempting to become sequestered in an ivory tower. In smaller agencies where staff is minimal or non-existent, this means little or no work might get done.

To overcome this obstacle, you need the three Ws in your board members: wisdom, wealth, and work. It is the rare person who brings multiple qualities in one neat package, but it's essential to have all three in varying mixes. Visionaries might get to create the agenda, but vision without action is a daydream. Workers can get the job done, but action without vision is a nightmare. Wealth is an extension of work, in that financial resources help the organisation accomplish goals which would be otherwise impossible or extremely cumbersome.

Set clear expectations which welcome vision, but not to the exclusion of action. Effectively use those who are task-oriented but not capable of rising fully to the level of strategic leaders.

Shadow Dancers

Similar to No Shows, these are board members you have to constantly prod into action as they avoid fundraising, making commitments, and, in the extreme, just plain don't show up. They render meeting quorums an issue and raise blood pressures needlessly. We also call them avoiders.

Oftentimes, they will say they are busy - but with the ongoing evolution of social media we now have insight into their activities and priorities. It can be nerve wrecking to see a board member post for hours each day on Facebook when they've told you they don't have

time to fulfill their fiduciary
commitments.

Dealing with avoidance means addressing
the underlying issues. Shift board
members to advisory boards where it
makes sense. If members lack the skills
to carry out a task, help them via
training. Lastly, develop a good
feedback mechanism by placing deadlines
in writing and sharing them with the
team.

Of course, none of this is likely to
resolve the issue of members who
changed their minds and simply decided
not to tell you.

Order Takers

Generally lacking initiative, these board members may be good workers and provide value but need to be told what to do -again and again and again. Though reliable and a welcome counterbalance to process with action drones, it can become a counterproductive cycle unless procedures are documented and readily accessible. Even so, well documented procedures need to be reinforced, becoming a stressful effort to guard against dropped balls.

In seeking inner peace, consider the balance of order takers and those more inclined to advise but not do. Every organisation needs people to create plans and help carry out them out. While you may hope for both in one package, get on with the reality of what you have to work with. 'Trust but verify' becomes the operational imperative.

Conflict of Interest

Everyone has an agenda. The hope is it's closely aligned to the mission of the organisation. Usually, the best time to determine them is during candidate interviews, but sometimes you're desperate for help or they say what you want to hear. Once on the board, their agenda become clearer.

Sometimes it is to recommend friends for positions or projects. Or board members who try to resuscitate old glories which are tangential to the mission. Each situation is unique, and dealing with conflicts of interest begins with the understanding that perceptions matter along with outcomes. A recommendation may have the appearance of conflict while still being the best choice. In cases where there is no exceptional benefit, it's best to avoid the conflict. In the end, it is about managing agendas for the

benefit of all concerned.

V.   Are We Done?

We all know we're not, and can probably write an epistle about the numerous situations in which boards or its members behave in counterproductive and nerve-wrecking ways. If you're so inclined, send me your thoughts and suggestions and let's continue the conversation.

Some might characterise this work as unduly negative, but a bit of shared angst is merely a precursor to the real thrust. Identifying and acknowledging limitations or weakness is the first step towards creating solutions. When setting about this process, it's

important to remember board leadership
is a challenging yet noble undertaking.
Its best rewards are reaped when one
stays the course despite the bumps and
disagreements which can occur. There is
a great deal one can learn about other
members of the team, the organisation,
and community members when in service
to important causes. If you're
fortunate, there are even lifetime
friendships which can be formed,
further enriching our lives.

Go out there and change the world!

www.ingramcontent.com/pod-product-compliance
Lightning Source LLC
Chambersburg PA
CBHW071622170526
45166CB00003B/1159